GOLF BALLS

THE FUNNIEST GOLF JOKES

JAMES CONRAD

I

James Conrad has asserted his moral right to be identified as the author of this work in accordance with the Copyright, Designs and Patents Act 1988.

Published by Blue Yonder Books

CONTENTS

INTRODUCTION

Golf is a peculiar game enjoyed by so many but mastered by so few. As the great transatlantic journalist Alastair Cooke noted;

In golf, humiliations are the essence of the game.

It is sometimes a long journey from the great hopes and expectations of the first tee to the cruel reality of the eighteenth hole.

This book cannot compensate for the twists and turns of cruel fate but hopefully will make a golfer's journey more enjoyable.

It is a collection of what, in the author's opinion at least, are the best golf jokes. I hope you enjoy them as well.

CHAPTER 1: THE WIFE

A PROVISIONAL

Fred's wife had recently died. He recounted the whole sad story to the coroner.

"We were on the third hole. I was about to drive off and my wife Sally was standing on the lady's tee, about 30 yards ahead of the men's box when I hit my drive.

From the sound when the ball hit her head and the way she dropped like a rock, I knew immediately that she was dead. God only knows where the ball wound up."

The coroner replied "Yes, that explains the injury to her head, but what about the Titleist embedded in her rectum?"

"Oh," said Bill. "That was my provisional. I wondered where that had got to".

BSE

It was during the height of the mad cow crisis that a man and his wife were playing a round of golf. After they had finished, they thought it would be very pleasant if they went in the club house and stayed for a meal.

The man was perusing the menu and the waiter came over to take the order.

"I will have the roast beef" the man said.

The waiter hesitated before writing it down. "But what about the mad cow" he asked.

"Oh, she'll have the same" the man said.

RECONSTRUCTION

Bill was driving to a golf tournament when he was in a terrible car crash. He was attended to by paramedics, and they managed to save his life but couldn't save his manhood which was mangled beyond repair.

The doctor said the situation could be repaired but unfortunately, the health service wouldn't pay for it as they viewed it as cosmetic.

The doctor informed Bill that there were three prices. Firstly, a small one would cost £2,000, a medium one would cost £6,000 and for a large one the cost was £12,000.

Bill was wondering whether he could afford the money for a large one, a small one was out of the question. "Why don't you phone your wife to discuss it" suggested the doctor.

So, Bill went next door and phoned his wife. He came back looking very dejected.

"What is the matter" asked the doctor.

"She's decided she would rather have a new kitchen" replied Bill.

A HEIFER

Bill staggered into a hospital emergency room, battered and bruised. A doctor rushed over to help him to an examining room.

"How did you receive these injuries?" the doctor asked.

"I was playing golf with my wife," Bill replied.

The doctor was incredulous. "How could you possibly have been injured this severely playing golf with your wife?" he asked.

Bill explained what happened.

He and his wife both hit their tee shots on the first hole off- line. "I hooked mine into the woods, left," Bill said, "while my wife hit a huge slice that flew into a cow pasture on the right side of the hole."

Bill explained he found his ball and hit it back onto the fairway, and then he went to help his wife locate her tee shot.

"I was walking around among the cows," Bill explained, "when I spotted something white on the backside of a heifer. I went over to it and lifted its tail, and sure enough, my wife's ball had lodged right in the heifer's posterior".

"So, I pointed at the heifer's backside and yelled over to my wife, 'Hey, honey, this looks like yours.' "

Voodoo

Jack was just about ready to tee off on the first with the lads on a Saturday morning when he got a phone call from his wife.

"Hello Darling how can I help you" Jack said.

"Do you believe in voodoo dolls?", the voice at the other end of the phone asked. "Like if someone sticks a pin in the doll then the person feels excruciating pain".

"No, of course not Dear" said Jack. "It is a load of nonsense"

"OK" the voice on the phone responded, "how about now"?

Arguing

Bob was arguing with his wife. "Do shut up, you are driving me mad" said Bob.

"That wouldn't be a drive" said Bob's wife, "that is just a short putt".

The Masters

Bill was lucky enough to get two of the best seats for the Masters. After he had sat down at his seat a man came up and asked if the seat next to him was vacant.

"Yes, it is." Bill said.

"That is amazing" said the man "that someone gets a fantastic seat for the Masters and doesn't come".

"Well," said Bill "I always used to come with my wife but unfortunately she died. This is the first one we haven't been to since we got married 45 years ago".

"That is terrible. I am so sorry" said the man. "Couldn't you get any of your friends to come instead".

"No" said Bill. "They are all at the funeral".

THE FLOWERS

Two wives were in a restaurant discussing the merits of their husbands.

"My husband is wonderful" said the first. "Every time he goes for a game of golf, he brings me a bouquet of flowers when he comes back".

"I hate flowers" said the second.

"Why is that? Flowers are beautiful. How can you hate flowers"?

"Yes, but every time he brings me flowers, he expects me to…you know" explained the second.

"He expects you to… what?"

"He expects me to spread my legs" she explained.

The first woman was horrified. "Oh my God, don't you have a vase"?

Telephone Call

The golfers were introducing themselves to each other on the first tee at the monthly medal.

"How do you feel about hearing lots of swearing, foul language and abuse" said one of the golfers.

"Fine" said another. "It will be like water off a duck's back to me. There is nothing I haven't heard before".

"That's good" said the golfer. "Can you ring my wife and tell her where I am?"

The Happy Couple

The happy couple were approaching the altar and the groom turns to the prospective wife and says:

"Honey, I have got a confession to make. I am a golf nut and will be playing at every opportunity".

"That is fine" said the wife to be "but I have a confession as well... I am a hooker".

"That is Ok" said the groom. "All you have to do is keep your head down and left arm straight".

Playing With The Wife

Fred was an excellent golfer and had decided he would play in the mixed doubles with his wife. Unfortunately, Fred's wife does not play very often and is not very good at the game.

Anyway, they start at a par 4 first hole and Fred decides to drive off. He splits the fairway with a 300-yard drive.

His wife plays the second shot and shanks it straight into the rough.

After a minute or two searching for the ball Fred finds it. He then plays an amazing recovery shot 15 foot from the pin.

His wife gets to the green, lines up the putt, and after due deliberation hits it 25 feet past the hole.

Fred then holes the long putt. On the way to the next hole his wife hears him grumbling to himself.

"What is the matter with you" she asks.

"Well, if we are going to win this tournament, we will have to do better than getting fives on par fours" Bill explained.

"Well, that's not my fault" his wife said. "You took three shots and I only took two."

THE WIDOW

Rita's husband Fred had sadly died, and she went to the local newspaper to put his obituary in the paper.

"How much does an obituary cost" she asked the man at the desk.

"It depends how many words you use" said the newspaper man.

"Well," said Rita "just let's just say 'Fred Brown dies'.

"I am afraid there is a minimum of seven words" said the newspaper man.

Rita thought about it for a minute or two and said "Okay, let's make it –

'Fred Brown dies. Golf Bag for sale'."

SILENCE IS GOLDEN

Bill and Tom were chatting while they were playing golf.

"Do you know my wife hasn't talked to me in over two months" said Bill. "I think I am going to divorce her".

Tom looks at him and takes a big intake of breath. "I would think it over very carefully if I were you" he said, "a woman like that is hard to find".

THE DANCE

Joe took his wife down to the Annual Dinner and Dance at the golf club. When he gets inside the club there is a man putting on a fantastic performance on the dance floor.

He is doing break dancing, moon walks and back flips, the whole lot, in a fantastic display.

Joe's wife turned to him and said, "Twenty five years ago that man asked me to marry him".

Joe responded, "Looks as though he's still celebrating".

SMALL WORLD

Two men get to the course for a quick nine holes after work. They get to the tee and see two ladies playing ahead of them.

The ladies are terribly slow and one of the men says he is going to ask if they can play through. He goes halfway to the ladies and turns back.

The other man asked what was wrong. The man said, "I can't go up there that's my wife and my mistress."

So, the other man says he will go. He goes halfway and comes back. His partner asked what happened and the man replied, "Small world, huh?"

SILENCE

Steve and his wife were having an argument and as was usual with this couple they were giving each other the silent treatment.

As he was going to bed Steve remembered that he has a 7.30am tee off time in the morning and needed his wife to wake him at 6am.

Obviously, Steve didn't want to be the one to break the silence and lose the argument. So, he wrote on a piece of paper 'Wake me up at 6am' and put it next to his wife's bed.

When he woke up, he looked at the clock next to his bed and it was 8am, and he had missed his tee time.

Furious he went to his wife's bed and he noticed a piece of paper by the bed. It said, 'It is 6am. Wake up'.

THE DISCOVERY

Bill and Jim were in the changing rooms after playing 18 holes when Bill made a surprising discovery. Jim was wearing a bra.

Bill didn't quite know what to say but enquired diplomatically "How long have you been wearing that?"

Jim rolled his eyes and replied wearily "Ever since the wife found it in the glovebox".

THE RESERVE

A husband and wife were playing golf together when the wife suddenly asked, "if I died would you marry again"?

"No, of course not" replied the husband.

"Yes, you would, I know you would" said the wife. The husband conceded that he probably would.

"Would you let her sleep in our bed" asked the wife.

"Yes, I probably would" replied the wife.

"Well," enquired the wife "what about my golf clubs. Would you let her use my golf clubs"?

"No, I wouldn't do that" said the husband. "She's left handed anyway".

CHAPTER 2: THE MEDICAL PROFESSION

THE HEART ATTACK

A married couple are out for their weekly round of golf, enjoying a great day.

But on the ninth green, something terrible happens. The wife suddenly screams in agony and collapses to the ground.

"Oh no," the husband exclaims, "you're having a heart attack."

"Help me, dear," the wife implores, "please find a doctor."

The husband runs off as fast as he can to find a doctor. He returns to the green in a short while, picks up his putter, and lines up his putt.

His wife raises her head off the green and glares at him. "I'm dying over here and you're putting?" she asks incredulously.

"Don't worry dear," says the husband calmly. "I found a doctor on the second hole and he's coming to help you."

"Well, how long will it take for him to get here?" the wife valiantly asks.

"No time at all, everybody's already agreed to let him play through."

THE DENTIST

A husband and his wife went to the dentist first thing in the morning.

"I have an emergency extraction" he said. "Could you take it out immediately as I am on the tee at 10 o'clock. Don't bother with any anesthetic just pull it out".

The Dentist said, "That will hurt but as long as you are prepared to put up with the pain, I will do it".

"That is no problem" the husband said. Turning to his wife he said, "Show him which tooth hurts love".

THE DOCTOR'S ASSESSMENT

Bill and Jim were chatting in the club house and Bill said, "I went to see the Doctor today and he has told me I can't play golf".

"So, he's seen you play as well then" said Jim.

TEST RESULTS

Sam goes to the Doctor to get his test results. "I've got good news and bad news for you" said the Doctor.

"Ok" said Sam, "you had better give me the bad news first. Let's get it over with".

"I am afraid your test results weren't good, and you only have two months to live" said the Doctor.

"That is terrible" said Sam. "Please tell me the good news. What can be good news after that"?

"I am playing in a four ball this afternoon" replied the Doctor.

ILLNESS

Bob and Steve were playing a round together, but Bob wasn't his normal self and was playing badly.

"What's up with you then Bob", enquired Steve.

"I am worried about the wife" said Bob, "I think she is seriously ill".

"Why on earth do you think that" said Steve. "Has she been to see the doctor?"

"She hasn't been yet, but she is definitely hallucinating" explained Bob. "She says she's seeing other people".

STRESS

Bill was feeling stressed out and went to see his doctor. After listening to Bill's problems and anxieties, the doctor asks Bill if he plays golf.

"Yes, I do" says Bill.

"Well why don't you play a round with an imaginary ball. You will find you shoot a much better score, and it relieves any frustration and stress. You will be much happier" said the doctor.

Bill thought this an excellent idea and when he told Jim they thought it a good idea to play a round with both having imaginary balls.

The round went very well with both players achieving incredible scores.

On the 18th hole, a par 5, Bill was 250 yards from the green when he took his second shot. As soon as he played the imagined ball he started jumping up and down shouting "It's in the hole, an albatross."

Turning to Jim he said, "I win, you can't beat that".

Jim turned to Bill and said "No, I have won. I am afraid you played my ball".

THE TOOTH

Bill was due to be on the first tee at midday but woke up with terrible toothache. He called the dentist and organised a 9am appointment.

The dentist looked at the tooth and said, "I am sorry Bill I am going to have to take it out".

The dentist was then sorting out the needle for an injection prior to the extraction when Bill said "I am afraid I can't have a needle. It is against my religion".

"That is OK, said the dentist "I have some gas".

"I can't have that either" said Bill. "That is against my religion as well".

The dentist then offered to do it the old fashioned way and offered him a bottle of whiskey. "I wish I could" said Bill, "but I am on the tee in a couple of hours and playing with the club captain".

"Ok" said the dentist. "Here are a couple of Viagra. Take these and come back in half an hour. This isn't against your religion is it?"

"No, it isn't" said Bill. "Will it help ease the pain"?

"No", said the dentist. "But it will give you something to hold on to".

WINDY

A man had an unusual problem with a 7 iron. Every time he played a shot with a 7 iron, he would break wind.

This was beginning to get embarrassing for him, so he went to the doctor and explained the problem.

"That is interesting" said the doctor. "I have a set of golf clubs here, show me how it happens".

The man then swung with the 7 iron and broke wind. He did it again with the same effect and again and again.

"I know what to do" said the doctor, and with that he left the room.

When he came back, he had a long stick with a nasty looking hook on the end.

The man was very concerned about where the doctor was going to put this stick and timidly enquired of the doctor "What on earth are you going to do with that?".

"I am going to open the windows. It stinks in here" said the doctor.

THE CHASE

Two golfers are on the fourth green when a naked woman runs across the green just as they are about to putt.

She is being chased by two men in white coats, and one of them is carrying two buckets of sand.

This group is then followed by an old man. The golfers stop the old man and ask what is going on.

"She is a nymphomaniac" he explained "and we are trying to catch her".

"But why is the man running with two buckets of sand" one of the golfers asked.

"He caught her first last time" he explained. "He has a handicap this time".

THE MEMBER

Ryan had a personal problem that was affecting his golf swing. His penis was too long to enable him a proper swing of the club.

This was causing him terrible embarrassment and eventually he decided to go to the doctor. The doctor asked him to drop his trousers.

"There you are doctor, "said Ryan, "You can see my problem. What can you give me for it?".

The doctor thought for a few seconds and then said to come to the window.

"Do you see that red Ferrari over there" said the doctor.

"Yes, I do" said Ryan.

"Well, I will give you that for it.

DRINK OF WATER

A woman was so worried about her husband losing his temper on the golf course that she went to see the doctor.

"I have no idea what to do" she said. "Whenever my husband is on the golf course, he loses his temper. It is beginning to scare me".

"Ah yes" said the doctor, "I have seen this before. Take some water with you on the golf course. When your husband looks as though he is going to lose his temper take a swig of water and just keep swilling it round your mouth".

The woman was a bit dubious about this. "How does me having a drink of water help my husband keep his temper" she enquired.

"The water has no effect" the doctor explained. It is having to keep your mouth shut which does the trick".

Chapter 3: Religion

HEAVEN

Tom was a man of faith, and a man of the golf course. He played golf every Sunday religiously, but only after attending church services.

Tom was getting on in years, and one day after feeling ill, he said to his wife, "I sure hope there is golf in the afterlife.

His wife told him not to overreact with talk about the afterlife. "Go to church and say a little prayer," she suggested, "and you'll feel better."

So, Tom headed to church. As he kneeled at the pew, Tom whispered a prayer: "Oh Lord, thank you for everything - my health, my wife and my golf game."

"I hope that when I reach Heaven I can still play golf."

As soon as he finished, a voice thundered: "Tom, this is the Lord. I hear you and will answer your question. Do you want the good news or the bad news first?"

Tom was startled. "Well, give me the good news," he said.

The Lord replied, "The good news is that in Heaven, we have thousands of championship golf courses, play is never slow, it's always free and you will never lose a golf ball."

Tom was ecstatic, "That's wonderful. You've answered my prayer. But what is the bad news?"

The Lord replied, "You tee off tomorrow at 9 a.m."

THE GOLFING NUNS

Two nuns were playing a round of golf and they just finished as the sun was setting. They decided they would finish off a perfect day by having a glass of wine in the club house.

Anyway, one led to two and eventually they decided they had better get back to the convent. However, once they got there, they found it was all locked up for the night.

The first nun said "there is only one thing for it. We will have to climb the walls".

With that she helped the second one to get a foothold on the wall and clamber up to the top of it.

As she sat on top of the wall the second nun says, "I feel like a commando".

"Yes", said the first nun, "but where are we going to get one this time of night".

THE AFTER LIFE

Bob and Sarah had been married for many years and were concerned about dying. In particular, they were concerned about whether there was an afterlife.

They agreed with each other that whoever died first would come back and tell the other about what happens when you die.

Eventually Bob sadly died. A couple of months later he makes contact.

"Sarah...Sarah, is that you? Can you hear me?" he says.

"Is that you?" Sarah asks.

"Yes, I have come back to tell you what it's like, as we agreed" said Bob.

"What is it like" asks Sarah.

"Well, I wake up in the morning and have sex. I then have breakfast and have more sex. Go to the golf course and have sex again. I have lunch and then have sex all afternoon" said Bob.

"You must be in heaven" said Sarah.

"No" said Bob. "I am a rabbit on the golf course".

PRAYING

Ralph was playing a round of golf with his priest when they got to the first par three hole.

"I am going to take an 8 iron" said Bill. "What are you going to take".

The priest peered at the hole and said, "I am going to take a 7 iron and pray".

Bill hit his shot and the ball finished 10 feet from the pin, while the priest topped his shot and it just dribbled a couple of yards.

Ralph turned to the priest and said, "normally when I am praying I keep my head down".

GOOD DEEDS

Harry was a curmudgeonly old golfer who one day was struck by lightning on the course.

He duly arrived at the gates of heaven and St Peter asked what good deeds he had done to earn his way into heaven.

"Well," said Harry "once I gave a pound to a homeless person. I also gave a pound to a blind beggar and I gave a pound to a woman who had lost her purse".

St Peter went to the Lord to ask what he should do, and the Lord said, "Give him his 3 pounds back and tell him to go to hell".

GOLFING HEAVEN

Three men were tragically killed in a car crash on the way to the golf course. They arrived at the gates of Heaven and were chatting to St. Peter.

"Are there any golf courses in heaven" asked one of the golfers.

"Yes, there are" replied St Peter. "There is only one local rule you have to abide by though, and that is don't tread on the ducks. If you do it squawks and they all start up and it is a terrible noise".

The golfers were bemused by this but went off to the course and lo and behold there were thousands of ducks.

They began playing and it wasn't long before one of them stood on a duck. It duly squawked and set of a cacophony of sound.

St. Peter appeared with an ugly woman. "As you stood on the duck the punishment is that you must be handcuffed to this woman for eternity" he said.

The two golfers were taken aback by this but carried on playing. In time a second golfer stood on another duck and the noise started up again.

St. Peter appeared again with an even uglier woman. She was duly handcuffed to the second golfer for eternity.

The third golfer kept playing and tiptoed around the ducks. He carried on like this for a couple of months before St. Peter appeared before him again, but this time with a beautiful blonde girl.

"What have I done to deserve this" enquired the golfer.

"I don't know what you have done" said the girl "but I trod on a bloody duck".

MYSTERIOUS WAYS

Father Steve woke up one Sunday morning to find it was a beautiful day. This would be a fantastic day to play a game of golf he thought to himself, but he had to take Mass.

He decided he would go to play golf and rang the Associate Pastor to tell him that he was not feeling well and could he take Mass for him.

Father Steve got to the first tee and he was all alone as everyone else was at church. As he was about to drive his ball St Peter leaned over to the Lord and said, "You aren't going to let him get away with lying and not going to church are you"?

"No, I am not" said the Lord. "He will be punished".

With that Father Steve gave the ball a mighty whack on the 450 yard opening hole and it flew like a bird toward the green and dropped straight into the hole.

St Peter turned to the Lord and asked, "how is that punishing him Lord?"

The Good Lord responded, "who can he tell"?

THE BLONDE

George was tragically struck by lightening on the eighteenth hole and naturally went to Heaven.

He was stood at the gates of Heaven when St Peter came over to him.

"Hello George" St Peter said, "as a result of you leading such an exalted life, we will allow you a special bonus of a reunion with one of your old friends. Is there anyone you would like to see"?

"Well, I would love to see my old golfing mate Bill" George said. "I haven't seen him for three years."

"No problem" said St Peter and led George around a number of corridors till he came to a room.

George knocked on the door and went in, and there was Bill sat reading a book while having his head massaged by a beautiful blonde girl while she was moaning and whispering in his ear.

This seemed a little strange to George, but he ignored the girl and sat talking to Bill about the good rounds they had had together and catching up on old times.

Eventually George asked "Why is the blonde here? Is it because you led a particularly good and worthwhile life, and is it your reward?"

"No" said Bill. "I am her punishment".

THE GREAT SHOT

Tom was on the third tee when he sliced the ball horribly into the woods. He eventually found the ball which is behind a tree. He didn't want to drop a shot by calling it unplayable so decided to play it.

He took a huge swing hoping to get the ball out of the woods, but it struck the tree and ricocheted back and hit him on the head. He fell down stone dead.

He got to the Pearly Gates and St Peter came down to see him.

"I notice that you are a golfer" said St Peter. "Are you any good?"

"Well," replied Tom "I got here in two didn't I.

THE BEST

A Priest, a Minster and a Rabbi were chatting about who was best at their job.

"I know how to resolve this" said the Rabbi, "let us all go down to the golf course and see who can convert a golfer. Golf courses are full of sinners".

They thought this was an excellent idea and agreed to meet to compare their successes in a weeks' time.

A week later they all meet. The Minister said, "I found a golfer on the course and read to him from the Catechism, and he is coming to Communion next week".

They all congratulated the Minister and the Priest said "I also went to the course and spoke to a golfer about the Holy Word and he was so lifted up by what I told him that he let me baptize him".

They all congratulated the Priest. "How did you get on" the Minister and Priest asked of the Rabbi.

"Looking back" said the Rabbi "perhaps I shouldn't have started with the circumcision".

CHAPTER 4: SEX

FOREPLAY
Fred comes home from work and finds his wife in some sexy lingerie.

She says, "You can tie me up and do what you want with me".

So, Fred ties her up and goes to play golf.

THE PARTY
A beautiful woman arrived at the party and noticed a handsome man in the corner. She went over to him and introduced herself.

"Hello, my name is Carmen" she said.

"That's a beautiful name" the man replied, "how did you get that name".

"Well, I gave it to myself as they are the things that I like most in life – cars and men" she replied.

"What's your name" she asked.

"B.J. Titsandgolf" he replied.

BRIBES

Four friends meet up on the tee on a Saturday for a round of golf and were chatting about what they had to do to get away from their wives.

"I had to promise to take her shopping and buy her whatever she wanted" said the first.

The second said "Well I had to promise her a new kitchen to get here. It will cost a fortune".

The third said "I have promised that I will decorate the house upstairs and downstairs".

The fourth had remained silent but then said "Well once the alarm went off at 6 o'clock I elbowed her in the back and asked "Golf course or intercourse. She said 'don't forget your sweater'".

THE SIX INCHER

An elderly couple were playing together at the club's Annual Championship and doing very well.

It got to the eighteenth and the woman had a six-inch putt to win the Championship. She was extremely nervous and missed it.

On the way home the furious husband berated her for missing it.

"How could you miss it" he said. "It was smaller than my willy".

"Yes, it was" she said, "but it was a lot harder".

THE COUNSELLOR
Bill and Rita went for counselling after many years of marriage. The counsellor asked what the problem was.

Rita began and listed a whole litany of problems over the years of their marriage. She felt neglected, lonely, unloved and unlovable amongst many other complaints.

The counsellor listened intently as she went on and on. Eventually he got up walked around the table and grabbed her and kissed her passionately.

Bill watched surprised and eventually the counsellor returned to his seat while Rita sat down and buttoned herself up.

"That is what she needs" said the counsellor to Bill, "can you manage that"?

"Well," said Bill "I can drop her off Monday's and Wednesday's, but I am playing golf on Friday's".

A STUTTER
Bob was new to the club and went to play a round. He did not have anyone to play with but saw someone at the first tee and they seemed to be alone.

"W-w-w would y-y-y-y you mind if I j-j-j joined you" asked Bob.

No problem said the golfer and they played eighteen holes chatting as they went round.

"I can't help noticing that you have a stutter" said the golfer. "I used to have a stutter far worse than you. It was cured when my wife gave me oral sex for six days on the trot. You should try it".

"Y-y-y yes I w-w-w-will" said Bill.

Next week the golfer saw Bill and asked how he was doing.

"V-v-v very w-w-w well" said Bill.

"You didn't take my advice then" said the golfer.

"Y-y-y yes I d-d-d did" said Bill. "Y-y-y you have a l-l-l lovely h-h-h-house".

THE PILL
Linda was very bored with her husband as all he thought about was golf and wasn't the slightest bit interested in sex with her. Eventually she went to the doctor to see if he could solve her problem.

The doctor listens patiently and gives her a pill. He tells her to slip that into his mashed potato and that should do the job.

She goes back to the doctor the following week and says, "Doc that worked great. Five minutes after eating his mashed potatoes he threw everything off the table, tore

31

my clothes off and ravaged me there and then on the table".

"I am sorry" said the doctor, "I will get you a pill that is less strong".

"No don't worry about that," said the wife. "We just won't go to that restaurant again".

CUTBACKS
Phil and Graham were playing in a competition together and Phil wasn't playing very well.

"What's the problem" asked Graham.

"Well, it's the wife" Phil explained. "She has taken up golf and now she has cut our sex down to once a week"

"You're lucky" said Graham. "I know two guys she has cut out altogether".

GAY
Keith and Brian were out on the course and Keith said that rumour had it that one of their golfing mates was gay.

Brian said "I hope it's Phil. He's real cute".

THE MILKMAN
Brendan came home from golf looking a bit flustered.

"What's wrong with you" asked his wife "you seem very anxious. Didn't the golf go very well".

"No, the golf went fine" said Brendan. "It was in the bar afterwards. The milkman was in there and said he had had sex with every woman in our street bar one".

"Ah, yes" said his wife. "I bet it is that stuck up cow at number 14".

THE MASTERS

A couple were sat in a stand at Amen Corner watching the Masters. The wife nudged the man in the ribs and said to look at a young couple sat a few rows away.

They were being very affectionate, and their hands were all over each other.

"I don't know whether to watch them or the golf" said the wife.

"You are better watching them" said the man. "You already know how to play golf".

THE CHEAT

Laura was certain that her husband was cheating on her and it always happened after she had been playing golf with her pals.

She was so tired after golf that she fell into a deep sleep in the evening, and nothing would wake her till morning.

She thought that during this time her husband was getting up to no good.

After playing golf one day she decided to set a trap. She told the maid she could go home for the weekend.

That night when they went to bed the husband said he didn't feel very well and went to the bathroom.

'I know what you're going to do' thought Laura, so she got out of bed and went and got into the maid's bed and turned the lights off.

About 10 minutes later the door gently and silently opened and a man came in the room. He slid into the maid's bed and immediately started to have sex with Laura.

When he had finished he was panting and out of breath and Laura said, "You didn't expect to find me in bed here did you" and switched the lights on.

"No, I didn't, madam", said the gardener.

THE SABBATH

A young Jewish man was a good golfer. He discovered that by having sex with his wife prior to a round of golf he could knock two shots of his score.

However, he was also a very religious man and he was concerned about whether sex was work or play. If it was work, he wouldn't be allowed to do it on the Sabbath and add shots to his round of golf. If it was play, then there was no problem, and he could play his best golf.

He decided to go and ask the Rabbi as he would certainly know. He explained his quandary to the Rabbi and asked what the answer was to this problem.

"Well," said the Rabbi "I can definitely tell you that sex is play".

"Thank you very much" said the young man who had got the answer he wanted, "but how can you be so sure"?

"I know" said the Rabbi, "because if it was work my wife would get the maid to do it".

DEMOCRACY

Jack just wasn't getting as much time for golf as he would like. He was having to look after his kids and it was all getting too much for him.

He decided if he was going to have time for golf to play as he got older then he would have to have the snip. So, he went to see the doctor.

"I would like to have a vasectomy" said Jack.

"That is a big decision" said the doctor. "Have you discussed it with your family"?

"Yes, I have" said Jack. "We took a vote on it and it was 17 – 2 in favour of getting it".

35

THE DISCUSSION

Three women were having tea and discussing their sex lives.

"My husband is like a Championship golfer" said the first. "He has spent years perfecting his stroke".

Well," said the second "I think my husband is like the winner of a Formula 1 race. He gives me lots of exciting laps with twists and turns".

The third woman said nothing. "What is your husband like" asked the other two eventually.

"My husband is like a 100 meter Olympic sprinter" she finally declared. "He has got his time down to under 10 seconds".

CHAPTER 5: THE GOLDEN YEARS

FAILING EYESIGHT

Jim was a particularly good golfer, but his eyesight was failing which meant he couldn't see where he had hit the ball.

He went to his doctor and explained the problem. "I have a solution" said the doctor. "I have another patient who is 85 and needs exercise but has fantastic eyesight. Why don't you take him round with you and he can watch for your ball?

Jim thought this was an excellent idea and they met up on the first tee the following Saturday. Jim drove off and it felt like an excellent shot and disappeared into the distance, but he couldn't see where it went.

He turned to the old man and said, "Did you see it?"

"Yes, I saw where it went" he replied.

"Where did it go then" asked Fred.

"I forget" said his partner.

THE CHURCH SERVICE

The vicar was giving his sermon on a Sunday and the subject was forgiving your enemies. He asked the congregation "How many of you have forgiven your enemies?"

Half the audience put their hands up. "What only half of you" the vicar said. "How many of you have forgiven your enemies" he said in an even more demanding voice.

With that all the assembled shot their hands up, apart from Bill, who only went to church when the weather was too bad to play golf.

"Bill", said the vicar, "I realise the weather is terrible and you can't play golf but why can't you bring yourself to forgive your enemies?"

"I don't have any to forgive", Bill replied grumpily.

"That is wonderful. What a magnificent example to us all" said the vicar ecstatically. "How old are you Bill?"

"I am 98" replied Bill.

"That is marvellous" said the vicar. "Come to the front and tell us all how you have lived to 98 and don't have an enemy in the world".

Bill tottered to the front of the assembled and stood in front of the pulpit and said, "I outlived all the bastards".

BIFOCALS

Pat had just arrived at the golf course as Jim was coming off the 18th green.

"The greatest game I had ever played" said Jim.

Pat listened intently but couldn't help but notice that Jim's trousers were all wet and enquired what had happened.

"Well," said Jim "I got some new bifocals yesterday and it was the first time I had used them on the course. They made everything that was small, big and everything that was big, small".

"I could drive the small ball miles with my big club, and when putting I was hitting the small ball into a large hole".

"That's fantastic but how did you get so wet" Pat persisted.

"Well, I got to the 14th" explained Jim "and I needed a pee. I went behind the hut and was going to pee but saw a big one and a little one. I knew the big one wasn't mine so put it back".

THE PARROT

Alf used to play golf every day starting at 7.30am with his 3 mates. However, Alf wasn't very firm on his legs due to his great age and one day he fell into a bunker and broke his leg.

This meant that he couldn't play golf while he was stuck recuperating and was getting terribly bored at home.

His mates put their heads together and thought it would be a good idea to get Alf a parrot to keep him company and thought it would be something he could talk to and keep him company.

The following week one of them rang Alf and asked, "How are you getting on with the parrot?"

"It tasted disgusting" Alf said.

"What! You weren't meant to eat it. It spoke 16 languages".

"Well," said Alf "why didn't it say something".

FAULTY HEARING
Bill and Bob were on the first tee and about to drive and there was a queue waiting to follow them.

Bill bent over and put the tee in the ground. With that he rushed over to Bob and said, "I just did a silent fart. What do you think I should do?"

"I think you should change the battery in your hearing aid" replied Bob.

SENIORS DAY
There were three retired golfers playing on Seniors Day at the golf club.

The first golfer observed "Windy day isn't it?

"No" replied the second golfer "It's Thursday".

"So am I" said the third, "Let's go and have a beer".

THE GOOD LORD

Larry had just retired after years of working in an office and his doctor had suggested that he plays more golf to keep active.

He was getting checked up and the doctor said "Larry you may be 70 but you have the body of a 50 year old"

"I have the Good Lord leading me" Larry explained. "Do you know even when I go to the toilet at night the Lord just puts on the light to show me the way, and when I have finished, he turns it off".

The doctor was extremely impressed with this and rang Larry's wife.

"Larry is fine" he said "but I am impressed by his faith. Is it true that the Lord is putting the toilet light on for him at night"?

"Oh no" she said, "he's peeing in the fridge again".

TELLING YOUR AGE

Steve and Brian are two senior golfers and were playing a round together. Suddenly Brian says, "Tell me how old you think I am".

"Ok I will tell you precisely" said Steve.

"Go on then" said Brian "you will never guess".

"Open your mouth, wide" said Steve. He inspected his teeth, and then felt his forehead and looked deeply into his eyes.

Finally, he concluded "You're 87".

"That's fantastic" said Brian. "How did you know".

Steve explained, "We did the same thing yesterday".

MISSING HEARING AID

Howard was nearly hit by a ball on the golf course. The golfer came to apologise and said, "I shouted 'fore' but you didn't move".

Howard decided he had better go and get his hearing checked by his doctor. The doctor gave him an examination and investigated his ears and said:

"Howard, you have a suppository in your ear".

"Ah thank you" said Howard, "I know where I put my hearing aid now".

THE MILITARY

Two aging military men were starting a round of golf and chatting about things.

"When was the last time you had sex" said one.

The man thought about it for some time and replied, "It must have been about 1955".

"That is one hell of a long time" said his playing companion.

"Not particularly, it is only 20:15 now".

THE FAIRY

Fred and his wife Rita were in their 60's and playing their regular Monday round of golf together. Unfortunately, Rita's drive sliced off into the woods and they went off to see if they could find the ball.

They were searching in the woods when suddenly a Wood Fairy sprung up and said, "as you have been such an exemplary couple together all your lives I will grant you one wish each to celebrate a wonderful marriage".

This took the couple aback a minute. "Well," said Rita "I would love to go on a cruise ship with my darling husband and have a romantic trip of a lifetime around the world".

With that two tickets magically appeared in her hand.

"That is wonderful" said the Fairy. "What would you like Fred"?

Fred thought about it a minute and said, "I would like a wife 30 years younger than me".

Both Rita and the Wood Fairy looked in disappointment. "So be it" said the Fairy and waved her stick and Fred became 92 years old.

43

THE CALL GIRL

Larry played in a regular seniors four ball every Saturday and he hadn't turned up for the previous couple of weeks.

His mates were concerned at this and thought he must be getting a bit down at home rather than coming out to play golf. They discuss how they can get him back to fighting fit again and decide to hire him a call girl.

The girl duly turns up Larry's house and knocks on the door and he answers. The beautiful girl is stood there in a plunging figure hugging dress and says,

"I am he to give you super sex".

Larry thought about it for a moment and then said "I will have the soup. What flavour is it?"

THE GOLF SHOES

Jeff was 85 years old and had always wanted some soft spike golf shoes like Fred Couples would wear. Anyway, one day after finishing his round he saw some in the pros shop and decided to get some.

When he got home, he proudly put them on and asked his wife June if she noticed anything different.

"Nope" replied June.

Jeff was frustrated at this so rushed off into the bedroom, took all his clothes off apart from his shoes and went back into the kitchen.

"Bo you notice anything now" asked Jeff.

June looked up and said "Jeff what is different? It was hanging down yesterday. It is hanging down today and will be the same tomorrow".

"Do you know why it is hanging down" said Jeff.

"Not a clue" replied June.

"It is looking at my new shoes" explained Jeff.

"Oh" said June, "such a pity you hadn't bought a new hat".

AMEN CORNER

Bill was 75 years old and watching the final holes of the Masters with his young enthusiastic grandchildren.

Bill said wistfully to the children "It's not easy getting old. I suppose you are on your first round in life, and I am on my last round".

"No, Grandad" said one of the children "You are in the sudden death play-off.

FEELING YOUR AGE

Mary was 95 years old and not feeling very well so she decided to go and see the doctor. The doctor gave her a thorough examination and said;

"There is nothing wrong with you at all. Why don't you take up golf it would make you feel better, and you would look 10 years younger"?

"That is all very well" said Mary, "but who the hell wants to look like an 85 year old"?

CHAPTER 6: LADY PLAYERS

THE MEMBER

Three ladies were chipping up to the eighteenth hole when a man jumped out from behind a gorse bush, wearing only a paper bag over his head, and ran across the green into the club house. The ladies stand in astonishment at the size of his manhood.

The first lady says, "Well he is definitely not my husband".

The second lady stared at his manhood and says, "He's not my husband either".

"I will tell you what", said the third lady "he's not even a member at this club".

GOLF BALLS

Andy went to play a round of golf with a girl from the office. He popped into the pro's shop to buy some golf balls and put them in his pocket.

The girl stared at the obvious bulge as he came out of the shop. Somewhat embarrassed Andy explained "It's only golf balls".

"Is that a bit like Tennis Elbow?" the girl enquired.

TIGER WOODS

Tiger Woods drove his Ferrari down to his local club to have a practice round with some friends.

He was just on the first tee and ready to drive when a blonde woman came running up to him.

"Someone is stealing your car from the car park and driving off in it" she said.

"Did you try and stop them" asked Tiger.

"No, I didn't" said the blonde, "but I did get the number plate".

CAR TROUBLE

Sheila got home from her weekly game of golf and her husband said "You are late today. You are never normally late. What happened and why do you look so flustered?"

"I'm having trouble with the car" she replied.

"Car trouble? What sort of car trouble?" enquired the husband.

"Water in the carburettor" she replied.

"But you don't know anything about cars. How do you know it is water in the carburettor?

"I just do. Don't argue with me or I will get irritated. I am telling you that there is water in the carburettor" she said.

"Ok. I won't argue, just give me the keys and where is the car" the husband said.

"It's in the lake" she explained.

THE HARE

Three ladies were playing a round of golf and were on the 14th tee. One of them drove off and gave the ball a mighty blow which sailed down the fairway and hit a hare on the head.

The woman was extremely concerned for the poor animal and rushed down the fairway to find out its condition.

When she got there, she found the animal was stone dead. This upset the ladies greatly.

One of the women said not to worry as she knew what to do. She rummaged in her golf bag and pulled a can of spray from it. She walked over to the deceased hare and sprayed it up and down with the contents of the can.

Miraculously the hare then sprung to life and ran fifty yards down the fairway stopped, turned around, and waved to the ladies. It then did the same again and again running 50 yards and waving to the astonished ladies.

What on earth was in the can the lady's partners asked. She turned the can around, and it said, "Hair spray. Returns life to dead hair with a permanent wave".

THE FROG

A woman is playing golf and her first drive on the first tee slices horribly into the woods. She is despondent but treks after it and starts looking for the ball in the undergrowth.

She doesn't find the ball but does come across a beautiful green frog which is caught in a trap.

"If you free me from the terrible trap, I will grant you three wishes" said the frog.

The woman was somewhat surprised by this but freed the beautiful frog to claim her three wishes.

"Thank you, Lady" said the frog. "There is a condition to the granting of your wishes".

The woman was curious about this and asked what the condition was.

"The condition is", explained the frog, "that whatever you wish for your husband gets the same increased by a factor of 10".

"That is fine" said the woman. "My first wish is that I am the most beautiful woman in the world".

With that there was a puff of smoke and she was transformed into the most beautiful woman in the world.

"For my second wish I would like to be the richest woman in the world" said the woman.

With that there was another puff of smoke and she was the richest woman in the world.

"Remember that your husband will be ten times more beautiful and richer than you", said the frog. "What is your third wish".

"Ah yes my husband", said the woman. "For my third wish I'd like a mild heart attack".

EARLY

Two lady players were discussing their husband's personal problems, as they are wont to do, while playing a round of golf.

"My husband has premature ejaculation" said the first.

"Oh dear," said the second "is there anything that can be done".

"Well, he has had an operation" said the first, "but it is still touch and go".

CHAPTER 7: THE GREAT GAME

THE ISLAND

Jim is in a plane crash and is the lone survivor on a desert island. He comes round and sees this beautiful girl looking at him.

"Thank God, I have been rescued" Jim says, but the girl says, "No I have been stuck here for two years".

"Why don't you come and stay at my house" she suggests. "You have a house" Jim asked.

"Yes, I built it" she replied. Jim went to the house and was amazed. It had bedrooms, a living room and a kitchen and was a fantastic home.

"Would you like a steak?" the girl asked. "You have cattle as well" Jim asked. "Yes, I have a small herd" she replied.

"Perhaps you would also like a beer with your steak. I brew my own beer as well", she said. Jim's amazement knew no bounds.

After Jim had eaten his steak and drunk his beer the girl said "I have been on this island for a very long time. Would you like to play around?"

He said, "You've built a gold course as well?".

THE IMMOVABLE OBJECT

James was playing the monthly medal and needed a good drive to keep in contention. He wound himself up and took a huge swing with the result the ball sliced horribly going over some trees and onto the next fairway.

He heard a scream go up and rushed to see what had happened. There was a man lying unconscious on the floor with a large bump on his head.

"What should I do" James asks his partner.

"Don't move him" his partner instructed. "If we leave him where he is then he is an immoveable object. That means you can play the ball as it lies or take a drop two club lengths away".

TEEING UP

A man was driving to the course to play golf in his Rolls Royce but was getting low on petrol, so he pulled over into a garage to fill up.

The pump attendant filled the car up and the man asked the attendant how much it was.

"One hundred and seven dollars 28 cents" he said.

The man took one hundred dollars out of his wallet and dug into his pocket and pulled out a load of change.

"Take the seven dollars 28 cents out of that" he said handing it over to the attendant.

The attendant looked at the contents of the man's pocket, and there were lots of golf tees mixed in with the change.

"What are these for" enquired the attendant holding a tee.

"There for putting your balls on when you drive off" said the man.

"Geez" said the attendant "Rolls Royce think of everything".

THE TREE

A young man thought he could get a quick nine holes in after work before it got dark. He was on the first tee ready to drive when an old man came up and said would he mind if he played with him.

The young man was a bit dubious but too polite to do anything but say yes. As it turned out the old man didn't hit it very far but was pretty quick.

They got to the ninth hole and the young man had a difficult shot. He had knocked the ball behind a huge pine tree, which obstructed his route to the green.

He was pondering his shot for a couple of minutes when the old man piped up "when I was your age, I would have taken an 8 iron and hit it over the pine".

The young man could recognise a challenge when he saw one and got his 8 iron and gave it a whack.

The ball hit the top of the tree and landed back down not two feet in front of him.

The old man looked at him and said, "the tree was a lot smaller when I was your age though".

THE COIN TOSS

Brian and Jim were due to play golf on Sunday and Jim was 15 minutes late.

When Jim got there Brian asked why he was late.

"Well, it is Sunday" Jim explained, "and I had to toss a coin as to whether to go to church or the golf course".

"That should only take a minute, why did it take so long" Brian enquired.

"I had to toss it 15 times" said Jim.

DIFFERENT CULTURES

An American and a Scotsman were discussing playing golf during the winter weather.

"We don't play during the winter" said the American.

"We play whatever the weather "said the Scotsman, "even if there is snow on the ground".

"Do you have to paint your balls black asked the American.

"No" said the Scotsman, "we wear a sweater".

The Tannoy

A man was about to play his shot on the first hole when a voice came over the tannoy;

"Would the gentleman on the first hole please play from the Men's tee box and not use the Ladies ".

The man backs off from his shot and looks over irriated at the tannoy. He regains his composure and addresses the ball again. Yet again the tannoy starts up;

"Would the gentleman please refrain from driving from the Ladies tee box".

He backs away again and starts to address the ball. The voice over the tannoy starts again;

"We really need the gentleman on the first Ladies tee to use the Men's tee".

With that the golfer was very irritated and turned and said;

"I would really appreciate the announcer being quiet while I play my second shot".

The Pro

Bill is playing a round with the club pro and duffed his first tee shot into the woods. He then proceeded to hit a tree which catapulted the ball across the fairway into another wood. Finally, after several more swings he finished up in the bunker.

All the while the club pro had stood watching what was going on without flickering.

"What should I do now" asked Bill.

"I don't know," said the pro. "What game are you playing"?

THE WEATHER

Jim was going to play golf the next day but was worried about the weather. He decided he would invest in a weather forecast for the golf course area, so he rang the Meteorological Department.

He gave the meteorologist the location of the golf course and he said "There is a 1% of chance of rain on the golf course when you are playing tomorrow".

Jim was much more relaxed after that and went off to play golf and was duly soaked. The next day a furious Jim rang the meteorologist to demand his money back.

"You said that there was a 1% of rain" said Jim.

"Was I wrong" replied the meteorologist.

Chapter 8: The Moral Game

The Wise Student

A group of students were asked what they would like to be when they left school.

"I would like to be a golfer" replied one student.

"Why is that?" asked the teacher.

"Because golfers have lots of fun" replied the student. "They don't need to be any good at golf, they don't have to practice or revise unless they want to, and best of all they get to keep their own scores".

The Modern Man

Jane was pregnant and she was going to pregnancy classes and wanted Frank to go along. Frank was ever mindful that he should be a modern husband so felt it important that he should help his wife wherever possible.

When Frank got there the class was full of pregnant women doing exercises and practicing their breathing.

At the end of the class the instructor said "It is especially important to go walking for exercise. It would be particularly good for the lady's partners to go with them to encourage them".

Frank mused on this for a few seconds and then wanting to be helpful asked "That is a great idea. Is it alright if she carries a golf bag while we walk"?

THE CHEAT
Fred's wife asked why he didn't play golf with Jim anymore.

"Would you play golf with someone who kicked the ball to improve their lie sneezed when you were about to putt and cheated when keeping their score?", Fred replied.

"Well, no I wouldn't" said Fred's wife.

"Neither will Jim" said Fred.

PLAY IT AS IT LIES
There was no love lost between Brian and Pete and they didn't trust each other a bit, but they had been drawn to play against each other.

Anyway, they putted out on the third green and Pete said 'six' while writing down his score. "How many were you Brian?"

"I was six" said Brian "...no wait a minute it was five".

"Eight" said Pete as he was writing down the score.

"How can it be eight" enquired Brian.

"Well," explained Pete "you took seven strokes and I have added a penalty shot for improving your lie".

THE MOTHER-IN-LAW

Kevin was playing with Tony and was 200 yards from the green on the 18th.

"Look" said Kevin. "That is my mother-in-law standing by the club house and watching. I had better hit a good shot".

"Don't worry" said Tony. "You will never hit her from here".

THE DECEIT

A husband and wife were playing a round of golf together. When they got to the third tee the husband couldn't keep silent any longer.

"Look" he said, "I have to tell you I have been having an affair with your best friend".

"Don't worry about it" said the wife. "Let's forget all about it".

The husband carried on playing surprised and amazed with his wife's calmness with the situation.

When they got to the tenth tee the wife couldn't keep silent any longer.

"I have a confession as well" she said. "Long before I met you, I used to be a man".

The husband went ballistic.

"How could you be so deceitful" shouted the husband. "You've been playing off the Ladies Tee for years".

A SCOTTISH MULLIGAN

An American went to Scotland to play a round with some long-lost relatives. After a bad tee shot, he played a 'Mulligan' which sailed miles down the fairway.

"What do you call a Mulligan in Scotland" asked the American.

"We call it three off the tee" replied the Scotsman.

THE ACCIDENT

Three golfers were on their way to a golf tournament when they were involved in a terrible car crash and were all killed.

They were stood outside of Heaven's gates when St Peter came along.

"Good morning all" he said. "As you can imagine Heaven is a very big place and the first thing we have to sort out is transport. We do this by awarding transport according to how faithful you were to your wives".

Frank spoke first and said "I have always been totally faithful to my wife. She has been the only one for me".

"That is very good" said St Peter. "You will be driving a Rolls Royce".

Next was Harry who reluctantly said, "I am afraid I erred about 20 years ago and had an affair with my secretary".

"Very well" said St Peter. "You have made one mistake but were otherwise good. You will be driving a Renault".

Eventually it was George's turn. "I have always been a womaniser all my life. I couldn't tell you how many women I have been with during my marriage".

St Peter looked displeased and said, "You will have a bike to transport you".

A couple of months later George was out on his bike when he came across Frank with his Rolls Royce, and he was looking particularly miserable.

"Hi Frank, what's the matter" said George. "You've been driving this beautiful luxury car in Heaven. Why are you looking so miserable"?

"Well, I was just parked up" explained Frank, "and my wife went past me on roller skates".

BUTTERCUPS

A man was playing a round on his own and when he got to the 15th hole, and he sliced the ball horribly and it went flying into some scrub land.

When he got to his ball, he found it was surrounded by beautiful buttercups. He thought for a minute and then decided to give himself a one shot penalty and move the ball away from the flowers.

With that a fairy leapt from the buttercups.

"Thank you for moving the ball from the buttercups" the fairy said. "I will grant you a lifetime supply of butter as a reward for saving these beautiful flowers".

"That is truly kind of you" said the golfer "but where were you yesterday when I landed in the pussy willow"?

THE TEACHER
The teacher asked little Johnny if he knew his numbers.

"Yes, I do" he replied. "My father taught me".

"That's good" said the teacher. "What comes after three"?

"Four" answers the boy.

"What comes after Five" asks the teacher.

"Six" answers the boy.

"Well done" said the teacher. "Your father has done a good job. What comes after six"?

"I don't know" said Johnny. "My Dad is a golfer and doesn't count beyond six.

THE WATER HAZARD
A man was playing the par three 18th and hit the ball over the small water hazard and on to the green.

When he got to the green, he saw a man in ragged clothing sat with a rod and some string fishing in the hazard.

The man putted out and went over to the man and asked what he was doing.

"I am fishing" said the ragged man.

The golfer felt sorry for the man so asked him if he would like to come into the club house for a pint. The ragged man immediately accepted.

The golfer got the drinks in and sat down with the man. He was struggling to know what to say to him, so he started the conversation by asking;

"Have you caught many today"?

"You're the sixth" replied the ragged man.

THE GOLF SHOES

Jim's father had died, and he was going through his things to sort everything out. While doing this he came across a 30 year old stub for a repair of his golf shoes.

He looked in the phone book and the company was still operating. So, he went down to the shop and handed over the stub out of curiosity.

The man took the stub and headed to the back of the store. A couple of minutes later he came out and said "They will be ready next Friday".

HYPNOSIS

Linda was fed up with her husband constantly being on the golf course and not taking any notice of her. Anyone one day while he was playing golf she went round to the neighbour's house to console herself, and one thing led to another.

The next day, she was wracked with guilt and rushed round to the hypnotherapist's office.

"I have been faithful to my husband for 20 years" she explained "but yesterday I was unfaithful to him for the first time".

"I have the most terrible guilt. I just want to forget all about it. Can you do that for me"?

The hypnotherapist shaking his head says, "Oh no, not again".

THE LAMBO

Kevin was waiting for his boss at the golf club when he rolled up in a brand new sparkling Lamborghini.

Kevin said, "Wow what a fantastic and beautiful machine".

"Yes, it is" said the boss. "If you work really hard, put in all the hours that God sends, and strive to be the very best at what you do then I will be able to get another one next year".

THE FROG

Mike was playing a round of golf and was on the sixth hole. He did a good drive but when he gets to the ball there is a frog sitting next to it.

He is thinking which club to play when he suddenly hears 'ribbit 9 iron'. He looks round and can't work out who said it. He looks at the frog and it says, 'ribbit 9 iron'.

So, he puts the wedge away and takes out the 9 iron. He hits the ball 6 inches from the flag.

'That was amazing' thought the man. 'He must be a lucky frog'. So, he picks the frog up and takes it to the next hole.

"What do you think frog" Mike asks.

"Ribbit 3 wood" came the reply.

He hits a 3 wood, and it goes straight into the hole.

Mike thought this is my lucky day. I am going to Las Vegas to really cash in on this lucky frog.

He gets to the casino and asks the frog what to do. 'Ribbit $3,000 on 6 black'.

Mike plucked up courage and stuck the money on number 6 and lo and behold the money was soon flooding towards him.

He buys the best room in the hotel and sits the frog down and says to the frog "you have changed my life. How can I possibly repay you"?

The frog replies "Ribbit. If you kiss me, I will turn into a beautiful girl".

Mike thought why not given all that the frog had done for him. As soon as he kissed the frog it turned into a gorgeous 15 year old girl.

"And that your honor is the case for the defence'.

THE DEAF MUTE

A four ball was playing pretty slowly and there was a single player behind them who was being constantly held up.

Eventually, he approached them on a tee and handed one of them a card. The card said 'I am a deaf mute. Can I play through please'?

"No, you can't" said the man. "It is appalling that you should use a physical handicap like that to your advantage".

The four ball drove off and played on. Later in the round the four ball were on the green and one of them was about to putt when he was hit in the back of the head by a golf ball. He fell to the ground unconscious.

When he came round the first thing he saw was the deaf mute with one hand on his hip, and the other hand holding four fingers up.

CHAPTER 9: THE NINETEENTH

<u>**THE COINCIDENCE**</u>

Bill and Barry were in the clubhouse reminiscing over their rounds of golf that day when Bill said to Barry "I think I detect that you are Irish".

"Yes, indeed I am" Barry replied.

"Well would you believe it, so am I" Bill responds. "Where do you come from in Ireland".

"I come from Dublin. I used to live in McCleary Street" said Barry.

"Would you believe it" said Bill. "So, did I. Which school did you go to?"

"It was St. Augustine's Catholic School and I left in 1970" replied Barry.

"Would you believe it" said Bill in complete amazement. "So, did I. The Good Lord must have thrown us together here for a reason".

With that George walks in having finished his round of golf and orders a pint from Jim the barman.

"It's going to be a long night" Jim says, "the Murphy twins are drunk again".

IN THE WARS

Bill and Jim were in the Bar reminiscing about their rounds of golf.

Bill said, "My round was like World War 2 – out in 39 and home in 45".

"You did well" said Jim. "I played Civil War golf – out in 61 and home in 65".

A FAULTY MEMORY

A man was in the Bar having just finished a round of golf when a beautiful woman walked into the club house. As she passed him, she said, "Oh hello there" and went to sit across the room.

The man felt he remembered her but couldn't place her, and she kept exchanging glances as though she knew him.

Finally, curiosity got the better of him and he went over to her and said, "I am sorry, but do I know you"?

"Yes", she said "You are the father of one of my children".

With that it all came flooding back to the man. "You are the woman I met at the party here five years ago. It was the only time I have been unfaithful to my wife and we had sex on the eighteenth green. It ended with you flogging me over the groundsman's roller".

"No", said the woman. "I am your child's English teacher".

THE PET

Sam had been seriously ill and couldn't get out for his usual round of golf on Saturday and was feeling pretty fed up. His mates told him the best cure for this was to get a pet to keep him company.

So, Sam went down to the pet shop and look around all the different types of animals and eventually he bought one – a centipede.

He was really pleased with his newfound buddy and on Saturday afternoon he thought he would go down to the club house and introduce him to his mates who suggested getting a pet.

He said to the centipede in its box "Do you fancy going down to the golf club?"

There was no answer from the box.

"Do you fancy going to the golf club?" Sam asked again.

Still no answer.

"Do you fancy going to the golf club" Sam said loudly to the box.

Finally, an answer came from the box, "OK I heard you first time. I am getting my shoes on."

THE PIANIST

Callum had a new girlfriend and decided to take her out for an evening meal to the posh local golf club to impress her.

The waiter seated them next to the pianist. Unfortunately, Callum couldn't hear a word his beautiful new girlfriend was saying. Eventually he went to the pianist and asked, "Do you play requests?"

The pianist was very flattered by someone taking an interest in his performance at last and said, "Indeed I do Sir?"

"Well," asked Callum "can you play dominoes please"?

THE BLONDE

The blonde asked the bartender for a double entendre. As he gave her one, he asked if she had played a round.

THE OSTRICH

A man walked into the club house, followed by an ostrich. The waitress went over to him and asked what he would like to eat.

"I would like steak and chips please" said the man.

"I will have the same" said the ostrich.

"That will be £11.43" said the waitress. The man reached into his pocket and pulled out the exact change.

The next day the man and the ostrich go to the club and the man says to the waitress "I will have a burger and chips please".

"I will have the same" said the ostrich.

Again, he reaches into his pocket and pulls out the exact change.

This carries on for several nights running and the waitress could no longer hold back her curiosity. "How is it that you just reach into your pocket and pull out exactly the right change" she asked.

"Well," said the man, "I drove off from the sixth tee and hit the ball into the woods. While I was there looking for my ball, I found an old lamp. I rubbed it to see what it was, and a genie appeared".

"He offered me two wishes and my first wish was that whatever I had to pay for I could just reach into my pocket and pull the money out".

"That is clever" said the waitress. "That means you will have unlimited wealth and be able to pay for anything".

"One question though, what's with the ostrich" she enquired.

"Well," sighed the man, "my second wish was for a tall chick with long legs who would agree with everything I said".

THE GORILLA

The Steward arrived at the golf club to open up the club house at 8:30 and, much to his surprise he found a gorilla on the roof.

He rushed into the club and locked the door behind him. 'What can I do' he thought to himself. He began to look through the phone book for assistance.

Much to his surprise there was a phone number for a 'Gorilla Removal Expert'. He gave him a ring and within 15 minutes he was knocking on the door.

The Steward opened the door and there stood the Expert. He had with him a ladder, a baseball bat, a shotgun and the nastiest looking Pitbull you ever did see.

"What are you going to do" enquired the Steward.

"Well," said the man, "I am going to put the ladder up the building and then with the baseball bat I am going to knock the gorilla off the roof. Then my dog is trained to grab the gorilla by the balls, and it is then subdued enough for me to put it into the cage in my van".

"Excellent" said the Steward, "but what is the shotgun for"?

"That is for you" explained the man, "if the gorilla knocks me off the ladder shoot the dog".

FAMILY VALUES

Three men were in the nineteenth discussing their families.

The first man said "I have four sons. One more and I would have a basketball team".

"That is nothing", said the second man. "I have ten sons. If I had one more, I would have a cricket team".

" I have been the most fortunate" said the third man. "I have seventeen wives. If I had one more, I would have a golf course".

CHAPTER 10: GOLF MATES

CHARLIE

"It was a bad day at the course," a guy tells his wife. "Charlie had a heart attack on the third hole."

"Oh my God that is terrible." she says.

"You're telling me," the husband replies. "I had to carry Charlie all the way back to the club house".

"That must have been exhausting" said the wife.

"Yes" said the husband. " The worst part was I had to keep picking him up after I played each shot".

THE IDENTIFICATION

Bill, Jim, and Fred would play a regular three ball every week. One week though Bill had a terrible accident at home. His home was burned to the ground and Bill tragically died.

The next day the policeman called on Jim and asked if he could come and identify the body. Jim went along and when the sheet was pulled back, he couldn't tell so he asked the mortician to roll Bill over. He rolled the body over.

"No that isn't Bill" said Jim.

This surprised the policeman so he went to Fred and asked if he could identify the body. Fred went along and again asked for the body to be rolled over.

"No that isn't Bill" said Fred.

This surprised the policeman again. "Why don't you think that is Bill" the policeman asked.

"Well," said Fred "Bill had two arseholes".

"Two arseholes?" enquired the policeman

"Yes", explained Fred, "everyone knew Bill had two arseholes".

"Every time Bill went to the golf club folks would say 'here comes Bill with his two arseholes'".

SOUNDS FAMILIAR

Ralph and Brian were playing a round of golf together when Brian hits it into a deeply wooded part of the course.

Brian went to find his ball and shouted to Ralph he had found it. Ralph then heard six whacks coming from the woods.

When Brian re-emerged Ralph asked, "How many shots was that?"

"Three" replied Brian.

"But I heard six whacks while you were in the woods" pointed out Ralph.

"That would have been the echo" explained Brian helpfully.

FRESH AIR

Bill is playing with three mates at a new course. He tees up on the first hole and has a swing and completely misses it.

Unperturbed he has a second swing and misses again. He does it again a third time.

Bill turns to his mates and says "Wow, this sure is a tough course."

THE GIRLFRIEND

Two golfers were playing golf and chatting about their sex life.

"Do you know I never slept with my wife before I was married" said the first, "did you".

"I am not sure" said the second "what was her maiden name?"

THE PUTT

Three single men are on the tee with a beautiful girl. They all tee off and get to the green. The girl has a 20-foot putt for a birdie.

"This would be the first birdie I have ever had" she says, "and the one that helps me get it I will go home with tonight".

This gets the lads excited, and the first golfer looks at the putt and says helpfully that it will break from the right.

The second examines the putt even more closely and says no in fact it actually breaks from the left.

The third golfer walks over picks the ball up and says, "That's close enough, I will give you that one", and goes home with the girl.

THE WILL

Tom would play golf every Saturday with his three mates without fail. One Saturday they gathered at the club waiting for Tom to arrive and a message came through that he had died overnight.

The three friends were shocked at the news as he had seemed as fit as a fiddle. They all went to the funeral to support his widow Rita the following week.

Afterwards they were chatting to Rita and she said she would like them to come to the reading of the will as Tom had remembered them in it.

The three arrived at the solicitors and he began to read Tom's words.

"To my playing companion Brian, I leave my properties in Mayfair, to Pete I leave my properties in Park Lane and to Keith I leave my Oxford Street properties".

This news astonished the three friends as they had never really discussed work and what they each did. Somewhat embarrassed they approach Rita and say they didn't know Tom was so wealthy.

"He wasn't" Rita said. "He had a paper round".

SHOPPING

Brian was late for his golf match and his mates were wondering where he was. Eventually he rolled up.

"Where have you been"?

"It is the wife's birthday tomorrow and I had to get her a present" explained Brian.

His mates were curious to know what he had got as it would give them some ideas for that most difficult of tasks.

"She said that she didn't mind what she got as long as it had diamonds in it" said Brian, "so I got her a pack of cards".

AN AUDIENCE

Bill hadn't heard from Fred for a while so gives him a ring to see how he is doing.

"How are you doing" asks Bill.

"Couldn't be better" replies Fred.

"How is the golf going" enquires Bill.

"You won't believe it," said Fred "it is going fantastically well. Last time out I scored my lowest round ever, I drove the par four third hole and got a hole in on at the thirteenth. Everyone in the club house was talking about my round".

"Ok" said Bill "I'll call you back when you are alone".

THE GIRLFRIEND

George and Howard were playing golf when George confided he had a problem. "It's my son" he said. "He is good looking, he has a well-paid job, and he is very intelligent and kind".

"What is the problem then" said Howard, "that all sounds like good news".

"He doesn't have a girlfriend" explained George. "For some reason he can't seem to find the right girl. You know everyone Howard, I am confiding in you because I think you will be able to find someone for him".

Howard agrees to have a think about it and the following week out on the course, he says he thinks he has found a good match for the son.

"She is absolutely beautiful" he explains. "She is very smart and kind, has a good well paid job and she is a fantastic cook".

"That sounds perfect" said George, "but is she good in bed".

Howard shrugs his shoulders and says, "some say yes, and some say no".

THE ILLNESS

Two mates were out playing golf and walking down the thirteenth when one of them clutches his chest and collapses.

His mates immediately panics and doesn't know what to do. He eventually whips out his mobile phone and calls the emergency services.

"I think my friend has died" he said. "What can I do"?

"Calm down" said the operator. "Firstly, are you sure he is dead"?

The man thought about this for a couple of seconds and then takes out his 7 iron and whacks his prone mate across the head.

"Ok" said the man "He's dead, now what"?

IN THE EYE OF THE BEHOLDER

Steve and Phil were walking along the sixth fairway and chatting about their families.

Steve pulled out a photo of his wife and said, "she is beautiful isn't she"?

"If you think she is beautiful you should see my girlfriend" responded Phil.

"Why is she an absolute stunner" enquired Steve.

"No", said Phil. "She's an optician".

Chapter 11: The Irish

The Irish Widow

Many years ago, in Dublin a long suffering wife finally got fed up with her husband spending his whole time on the golf course and beat him to death with his own golf clubs.

The case came to trial and she pleaded guilty to the charge of murder. The judge began his sentencing and, as she had committed a capital offence, put his black cap on meaning she was going to be hanged.

He looked over to her alone in the dock and looked into her beautiful blue sorrowful eyes. Slowly he took the black cap off.

"I am going to be lenient with you" he said. "You are a widow after all".

A Bang on the Head

Murphy was playing golf when a ball hit him on the head.

The golfer ran up to see how Murphy was and full of apologies.

"That will cost you 5 grand" Murphy said.

"I shouted fore" pleaded the golfer.

"OK, I will settle for that", said Murphy

Logic

Paddy was playing in a regular foursome but had a new partner this day. On their way around the course Paddy asked the new player what he did.

"I am a Professor of Logic" said the player.

"That's incredible" said Paddy. "I never knew people got paid for doing that. What does it involve?"

"Well," said the Professor "do you have a doghouse".

"Yes, I do" said Paddy.

"I can infer from that that you have a dog" said the Professor.

"Yes, I do" said Paddy

"You probably also have a family" said the Professor.

"Yes, I do" said Paddy

"That will mean you have kids and are married" inferred the professor.

"Yes, I am" said Paddy.

"Well, said the Professor "from knowing that you had a doghouse I can logically deduce that you are a heterosexual".

Paddy marvelled at the power of logic. The next day he was playing with Murphy and explained that he had been playing with a Professor of Logic.

"What does he do" asked Murphy.

"Let me give you an example", said Paddy. "Do you have a doghouse?".

"No" said Murphy.

"Ah," said Paddy "so you are one of those gays".

KEEPING AHEAD

The golf club were having some major construction work done to the club house. However, four Irishman thought this would be no impediment to their game.

On the first tee Murphy was about to tee off. Suddenly there was a big crack on a crane lifting a girder. Immediately a girder swung across the first tee hitting Murphy and knocking his head clean off, like a football.

The other players were astonished and shocked at this development and didn't know what to do.

"I don't even know where he lived" said the first, "was he married"?

"Yes, I think I know where he lived" said the second. "I will go and see her" as he picked up the head.

He knocked on the door and held the head behind him. A woman came to the door.

"Hello, are you Murphy's wife" the golfer asked.

"Yes, I am" she answered.

"Is that the Murphy with red curly hair"?

"Yes, it is" said the woman.

"Does he have a scar above his right eye" enquired the golfer?

"Yes, he has" answered the woman.

The golfer then held the head up in front of the woman and asked, "Is this Murphy"?

"No, it isn't" responded the woman, "he is much taller than that".

FREE PINTS

A Scotsman, an Englishman and an Irishman were in the bar after playing 18 holes and reminiscing.

The Scotsman looked at his pint and said, "In Glasgow I would go to my local pub and the landlord would give me a fifth pint after I had bought four".

"I had something similar happen to me" said the Englishman. "When I was in London the landlord would give me a free pint after I had bought three".

"That's nothing" said the Irishman. "Back in Dublin the moment you walk in the pub they give you a pint straight away and kept giving you as many drinks as you can drink. Then they will take you upstairs and see that you have sex".

The Englishman and Scotsman were somewhat dubious about this and asked if this had actually happened to him.

"Well, no not to me personally" said the Irishman "but it has happened to my sister several times".

THE SQUEEZE

Murphy hadn't played a round for a while but decided he would go to get back in the swing of things with his mates.

He was on the first tee driving off and gave the ball an almighty whack. The ball flew 10 feet and hit Pat on the temple, and he fell like a stone.

Murphy rushed over to Pat to try to help but he seemed unconscious. Murphy grabbed Pat's hand and said "can you hear me? Can you hear me?"

"Squeeze once for yes, and twice for no".

WORK

Steve and Simon were playing a round of golf. Steve is a lawyer and said, "I think that my job is the best job you can get".

Simon was a bit surprised by this and asked "how on earth have you come to that conclusion"?

"Well," explained Steve "people come to my offices, tell me all their problems, and they pay me for my advice".

"Ah yes", said Simon " but in my job people come to my office, tell me all their problems and take their clothes off, and then pay me for my advice".

WHAT IS IN A NAME
Pat was playing in a big tournament and was on the first tee ready to drive. The announcer read out his name to the crowd;

"And now on the tee Mr. Pathogen".

Pat looked up and went over and whispered in the announcer's ear.

"I am sorry" said the announcer "and now on the tee Mr. Pat Hogen".

CHAPTER 12: GOLFING PARADOXES

How is it if we hit the ball into the rough, or the bunker or a water hazard everyone and their dog can tell us what we did wrong. However, if we happen to belt it down the middle of the fairway no one can tell us what we did right.

Why is it that we are perfectly capable of chipping a ball over a green and into a bunker, but totally incapable of chipping over a bunker onto the green?

You play your best golf when you don't try to hit the ball.

Why is it that slow groups are always in front of you and fast ones behind you?

There is no money back guarantee for golf lessons, no matter how terrible the result.

Why is it that the entire point of golf is to play as little golf as possible? The more shots you play the worse you are.

CHAPTER 13: QUESTIONS

Q: What do you call a beautiful girl on the arm of a golfer?
A: A tattoo

Q: What is the difference between a golf ball and the G spot?
A: A man will spend 5 minutes looking for his golf ball.

Q: What do you call a blonde golfer with an IQ of 130?
A: A foursome

Q: What do you call a woman who can suck a golf ball through a hose?
A: Darling

Q: What do golf and sex have in common?
A: They are two things you can enjoy without being any good at them

Q: What is the easiest shot in golf?
A: The fourth putt.

Q: What is the difference between a Ford and a golf ball?
A: You can drive a golf ball 300 yards.

Q: What do you do if you are in a bunker and hungry?
A: Get a sand wedge.

Q: You are trapped in a room with a lion, a tiger and the guy who shouts 'Mashed Potato' at tournaments. You have a gun with two bullets, which do you shoot?

A: Shoot the Mashed Potato guy twice.

Doctor: Do you play any sports at all?
Patient: Does sex count?
Doctor: Yes.
Patient: Then no.

Q: What has eight arms and an IQ of 45?
A: Four guys shouting, 'Mashed Potato'.

A woman answers the phone and a heavy breathing pervert says "I bet you have a tight ass and no hair"? "Yes, I do" said the woman. "He is watching golf. Who shall I say is calling"?

Chapter 14: Caddies

Golfer: Caddy why didn't you watch where my ball was going?
Caddy: Because I wasn't expecting it to go anywhere.

Golfer: You must be the worst caddy in the world.
Caddy: That would be a hell of a coincidence

Golfer: Golf is a funny game.
Caddy: It's not meant to be.

Golfer: Is there any improvement today?
Caddy: Yes ma'am. You've had your hair done.

Golfer: Can you go and get my ball from the pond?
Caddy: Why?
Golfer: It's my lucky ball.

Golfer: This can't be my ball. It is too old.
Caddy: We teed off a long time ago.

Golfer: Do you think my game is improving?
Caddy: Yes, it is. You are missing the ball much closer than you used to.

Caddy: We call where you hit your ball 'Lion Country'.
Golfer: Why is it called Lion Country?
Caddy: Because if you find the ball, you're 'a lion'.

Golfer: Do you think I can get there with a 5 iron?
Caddy: Yes, you will eventually

Golfer: Should I hit a half wedge?
Caddy: Yes, hit half now and you can hit the other half later.

Golfer: I think I am going to drown myself in the lake.
Caddy: Don't worry, you will be OK. You can't keep your head down that long.

Golfer: Have you ever seen a golfer worse than me?
Caddy: Yes, but they quit years ago.

Golfer: I would move heaven and earth to be able to shoot under a hundred.
Caddy: I would try heaven as you have already moved most of the earth.

Golfer: Do you think I can carry the bunker?
Caddy: I wouldn't have thought so. It must have 10 tons of sand in it.

Golfer: I have never played this badly before.
Caddy: I didn't realise you had played before.

CHAPTER 15: WORDS OF WISDOM

The best wood in a golfer's bag is the pencil.

No matter how bad your last shot the worst is still to come

If you are playing with a golfer who never cheats, then he is also a liar.

A 'gimme' is a mutually beneficial agreement between two poor putters.

There are only three ways to improve your golf game – take lessons, practice or cheat.

You can always tell if a player has missed the ball or just done a practice swing. Nobody swears after a practice swing.

The best sound in golf is the whooshing noise as your mate throws his golf club.

The great advantage that golf has over fishing is that golfers don't have to produce anything to prove their tall story.

To some golfers the greatest handicap is to add up correctly.

Counting on your opponent to inform you when he breaks a rule is like expecting him to make fun of his own hair cut.

Old golfers don't die. They just lose their balls.

The player with the fastest golf cart never has a bad lie.

The worse you play the better you remember the occasional good shot.

If you can't outplay them then outcheat them.

It is good etiquette to concede the fourth putt.

A golf cart is always preferable to a caddy as it can't laugh, criticize, or count.

If you use golf balls from the same sleeve, then they will tend to follow each other. This is particularly the case when water or out of bounds is involved.

Golf is a 5 mile walk punctuated with frequent disappointments.

The higher the handicap of the player you are playing with the more likely he is to tell you where you are going wrong.

Swing hard in case you hit it.

Work is for people who don't know how to play golf.

Whoever said practice makes perfect obviously never played golf.

A stroke does not occur till it is observed by another golfer.

Any swing change works for a maximum of three holes and a minimum of none.

Everyone replaces a divot after a perfect approach shot.

Never leave your opponent with the sole responsibility for thinking all the things that could go wrong with his shot.

No putt ever got longer as a result of being marked.

You know your golf game isn't good when you have to have your golf ball retriever regripped.

The ball always lands where the pin was yesterday.

The people who gave us golf and called it a game are the same people who gave us bagpipes and called it music.

The best golf partners are those not quite as good as you.

New golf balls are magnetic to water.

The more incompetent the golfer the more they see golf lessons as a weakness.

CHAPTER 16 GOLF QUOTES

In golf humiliations are the essence of golf.
Alastair Cooke

The only time my prayers are never answered is on the golf course
Billy Graham

Golf...is the infallible test. The man who can go into a patch of rough alone, with the knowledge that only God is watching him, and play his ball where it lies, is the man who will serve you faithfully and well.
PG Wodehouse

Golf is a fascinating game. It took me nearly forty years to discover that I can't play it.
Ted Ray

While playing golf today I hit two good balls. I stood on a rake.
Henry Youngman

Hockey is a sport for white men. Basketball is a sport for black men. Golf is a sport for white men dressed as black pimps.
Robin Williams

My swing is so bad I look like a caveman killing lunch.
Lee Trevino

Golf's three ugliest words; it's still your shot.

Dave Marr

The golf swing is like a suitcase into which we are trying to pack one too many things.
John Updike

Golf appeals to the idiot in us and the child. Just how childlike golfers become is proven by their frequent inability to count past five.
John Updike

I have a tip that can take 5 shots off anyone's game. It's called an eraser.
Arnold Palmer

Golf is so popular simply because it is the best game in the world at which to be bad.
A.A. Milne

I know I am getting better at golf because I am hitting fewer spectators.
President Gerald Ford

We learn so many things from golf – how to suffer, for instance.
Bruce Lansky

One minute you're bleeding. The next minute you're hemorrhaging. The next minute you're painting the Mona Lisa.
Mac O'Grady

Give me golf clubs, fresh air, and a beautiful partner, and you can keep the clubs and fresh air.

Jack Benny

The statute of limitations on forgotten strokes is two holes.
Leslie Nielsen

I don't exaggerate. I just remember big.
Chi Chi Rodriguez

The last thing you want to do is shoot 80 wearing 'tartan troosers'.
Ian Poulter

Why am I using a new putter? Because the last one didn't float too well.
Craig Stadler

Golf is the only game where a precise knowledge of the rules can earn a reputation for bad sportsmanship.
Patrick Campbell

Golf seems an arduous way to go for a walk. I prefer to take the dogs out.
Princess Anne

By the time a man can afford to lose a golf ball he can't hit it that far.
Lewis Grizzard

You can make a lot of money in this game. Just ask my ex-wives. Both of them are so rich neither of their husbands have to work.
Lee Trevino

I will always remember the day I broke ninety. I had a few beers in the clubhouse and was so excited I forgot to play the back nine.
Bruce Lansky

I would like to see the fairways more narrow. Then everyone would have to play from the rough, not just me.
Seve Ballesteros

I owe everything to golf. Where else could a guy with an IQ like mine make this much money?
Hubert Green

My favourite shots are the practice swing and the conceded putt. The rest can never be mastered.
Lord Robertson

The ball retriever is not long enough to get my putter out of the tree.
Brian Weis

ONE LAST THING

If you have enjoyed this book I would love you to write a review of the book on Amazon. It is really useful feedback as well as giving untold encouragement to the author.

If you have any comments, corrections, suggestions for improvements or for other books I would love to hear from you, and you can contact me at; jamesconradbooks@gmail.com

Your comments are greatly valued, and the books have been revised and improved as a result of helpful suggestions from readers

Printed in Great Britain
by Amazon

12818522R00061